Manual
for
Job-Communication
Satisfaction-Importance
(JCSI)
Questionnaire

Manual
for
Job-Communication
Satisfaction-Importance
(JCSI)
Questionnaire

Bonnie Weaver Battey, Ph.D. R.N.

To order additional copies of this book, contact:
Xlibris Corporation
1-888-795-4274
www.Xlibris.com
Orders@Xlibris.com
77541

CONTENTS

INTRODUCTION

The JOB-COMMUNICATION SATISFACTION-IMPORTANCE (JCSI) questionnaire is designed to survey large groups of nursing and other health care personnel in a hospital or similar agency. Information about perceived satisfaction and importance of selected aspects of the task and people associated with health care employees' work provides an excellent data base for administrative decisions. For example, such information may identify educational needs of personnel, areas of conflict to be resolved, and changes needed in areas deemed important to the personnel. In addition, the JCSI questionnaire can also reveal covert areas of success, such that excellence in performance may be appropriately recognized and rewarded, providing a strong role model for other personnel. There is some evidence that job satisfaction and successful communications have been associated with labor-management relations, productivity, and profit; all are desirable management goals in most organizations. In health care agencies, these concepts have been related to nursing staff turnover and retention.

PURPOSE

The purpose of the JCSI questionnaire is to determine the degree to which nursing and other health care personnel are satisfied or dissatisfied with their job and with the communication and interpersonal relationships existing among peers, supervisors, administrators and others. It also provides information about the degree of importance the personnel attach to these factors, thus identifying and prioritizing areas needing attention. The JCSI provides important data for purposes of research, management and consultation.

DEVELOPMENT OF THE JCSI QUESTIONNAIRE

The JCSI Questionnaire consists of 28 items which respondents are asked to rate on Likert scales their degree of perceived satisfaction-dissatisfaction and importance-unimportance about jobs-related issues. The questionnaire was derived from the initial efforts of Downs and Hazen (1977) and of Thiry (1977); Hazen, Thiry and Duldt were students of Downs at the University of Kansas in the early 1970's.

The specific topics included on the JCSI questionnaire were planned as follows:

Items 1-3: Overall job satisfaction, its general importance, and overall feelings of being successful.

Items 4-8: Communication generally.

Items 9-14: Communication about task.

Items 15-18:   Communication about interpersonal relations

among nursing staff members.

Items 19-24:   Communication and interpersonal relations

between immediate supervisor or superior,

subordinates.

Item 25:   Communications from the chief administrator

of the nursing service department within the

agency.

Item 26:   Communication from other departments.

Item 27:   Communication from physicians.

Item 28:   Communication from volunteers.

Items 1-3 are to be analyzed separately because these are designed to obtain a general, overall evaluation or perception by the subjects. Factor loadings and labeling of factors followed the questionnaire plan to some degree. See Tables 1-6. Table 7 presents comparison of factor labeling across several studies.

Optional open ended items 29-38 may be added, particularly in the context of consultation rather than research. These items request rather specific information and descriptions of the source of employee dissatisfaction:

Item 29:   Source of satisfaction.

Item 30:   Source of dissatisfaction.

Item 31:   Most important aspect of job.

Item 32:   One most preferred change wanted.

See the Appendix for the JCSI questionnaire and the specific items and scales.

Job Satisfaction

According to Herzberg, et. al., (1959), job satisfaction is a multidimensional construct composed of aspects of one's job about which one feels particularly good or bad. Herzberg's two-factor theory categorized these factors into the "motivators" (achievement, recognition, the task, responsibility and advancement) and "hygienic" factors (company policy, administration, supervision, salary, interpersonal relations with co-workers, and working conditions). Larson, et al. (1984) report that job satisfaction scores are predictive of nurses' job expectations and the importance placed on aspects of the work situation.

> " . . . organizational reasons for obtaining overall measures of job satisfaction relate either to using the results to reduce staff turnover and absenteeism or to improve the quality of the product rendered—in this case, patient care" (Larson, et al., 1984, p. 31).

There have been numerous investigations into job satisfaction of nurses. For example, in a study of RNs in long-term care facilities, Pfaff (1987) reports a set of factors similar to those of Herzberg's: satisfiers included achievement, recognition, the work itself, responsibility, and advancement; dissatisfies included facility policy, current job environment, salary, job security, peer interaction, and supervisor-staff relationships.

Communication Satisfaction

There is an increasing attention to communication in organizations as a specific focus of job satisfaction. The development of the construct, communication satisfaction, can be traced to Likert (1967), who identified communication as an intervening variable between organizational goals on the one hand and four desirable end results, i.e., productivity, satisfaction, labor-management relations, and profit.

Communication satisfaction is defined as an individual's satisfaction with various aspects of the communication occurring in his organization (Crino & White,1981). It involves "the personal satisfaction inherent in successfully communicating to someone or in successfully being communicated with . . ."(Thayer, 1968, p. 144).

Downs and Hazen (1977) developed an instrument with which they have identified eight factors of communication satisfaction: personal feedback, corporate perspective, organizational integration, relations with one's supervisor, the communication climate generally, horizontal communication, media quality, and relations with subordinates.

The JCSI is an adaptation of this instrument by Downs and Hazen and a similar research tool by Thiry (1977). Duldt has successfully used the JCSI questionnaire numerous times in consulting. In a research project involving

77 R.N. subjects, Duldt (1987) has identified the following six factors on the JCSI Scales: communication with immediate supervisor, personal job communication, communication with co-workers, communication with others, organizational job communication, and leadership. (See Appendix, Tables 1-6). Principal components factor analysis was used with a decision rule requiring each factor to have an eiguenvalue greater than 1.00. This analysis resulted in a six-factor solution accounting for 72.7% of the satisfaction scores, and in a six-factor solution accounting for 68.4% of the importance scores. To attempt to interpret and describe the cluster of job-facet items forming each factor, descriptive factor titles were assigned. Each item was assigned to a factor only once.

In reviewing the research which has been reported on communication satisfaction, Pincus (1986, p. 20) states:

"Interestingly, the body of non-nursing organizational literature demonstrates clearly the important contribution of different types of organizational communication to job satisfaction. Interpreted broadly, communication, which encompasses both information exchange and relationship-building elements, touches—and can affect—all the factors comprising job satisfaction. Nurse and hospital executives, therefore, must be sensitive to the communication atmosphere in their organizations because of its potential impact on nurses' job satisfaction and job performance."

Based on his own factor analytic study, Pincus (1986) identified nine communication satisfaction dimensions, all of which positively and significantly correlated with job satisfaction. The three most significant communication factors identified were communication with one's supervisor, communication climate, and personal feedback. The job satisfaction factors which were most strongly influenced by communication factors were the communication in the superior-subordinate relationship, the communication with top-level management, and the peer relationships or horizontal communication. A study by Thiry (1977) of public health nurses in Kansas yielded similar findings. In contrast, it is noteworthy that communication in interpersonal relationships was classified as a hygienic factor by Herzberg. (See Appendix, Table 7 for a chart comparing factors identified by each of the investigators.)

The Holistic and Humanistic Paradigms

Concurrently, holistic and humanistic paradigms are developing both in the health care arena and in the leadership and management arenas. In health care, an ancient nursing paradigm is being revitalized, that of humanistic nursing (Duldt, et al., 1984, 1985). Situational Leadership theory exemplifies the merging of behavioral, holistic, and humanistic world views as applied to leadership and management (Hersey and Duldt, 1989).

A common focus of these paradigms is on communication behaviors conveying caring and, consequently, on interpersonal communication. Interpersonal communication is the humanizing element which involves one person developing sensitivity or an awareness in another person of a wide range of human sentiment, characteristics, potential, capabilities, creativity, attitudes and values. Stewart and D'Angelo (1975) state:

> The quality of our interpersonal relationships determines who
> we are becoming as persons. Interpersonal communication is not
> merely one of many dimensions of human life; it is the defining
> dimension, the dimension through which we become human.

Both supervisors and nursing staff have a shared responsibility for what is happening in the interactions occurring between them. Through dialogue with the supervisor, the nursing staff can be influenced and afforded the opportunity to actively participate in the development of preferred communication attitudes (values), knowledge, and skills. Thus, interpersonal communication is an essential component for nursing leadership.

A fundamental tenet of humanistic nursing and leadership theory proposes that humanistic individuals demonstrate behaviors indicative of a sensitivity or awareness of the holism, the synthesis of the mind, body and spirit. So, when nursing supervisors demonstrate humanizing leadership behaviors, one would theoretically expect a higher than normal probability that their nursing staff would practice holistic and humanistic nursing, too.

However, very little is known about the nature of interpersonal communication occurring between supervisors and their nursing staffs. Carter (1982) found nursing staffs to be healthier than their liberal arts peers, but Meissner (1986) believes nurses eat their young, and Dr. Vernice Ferguson (1988) urges nurses to "tipping the scales" in favor of our young.

THEORETICAL BASIS OF RESEARCH

It is important to each discipline to develop its own knowledge base by verifying its theories through research. In accord with this expectation, the JCSI has been developed within the parameters of Duldt's Humanistic Nursing Communication Theory and is believed to be consistent with the holistic and humanistic paradigms. Its focus is on the leader-follower interpersonal communication existing between supervisors and their nursing staffs. For example, in considering Duldt's Humanistic Nursing Communication theory, the theoretical definition, humanizing communication, would logically include the communication aspects of job satisfaction as described by Herzberg, i.e., communication satisfaction. In a similar fashion, the scope of dehumanizing communication would include those interpersonal communication aspects of job dissatisfaction. If the JCSI questionnaire is used with the Nursing Communication Observation Tool (NCOT) within the theoretical framework of Humanistic Nursing Communication theory, a wide range of communication data can be obtained for purposes of research, management, and consultation.

It is believed those supervisors' and nursing staffs' self-reported job-communication satisfaction-importance would tend to be closely correlated. An example of research proposition which may be tested as adapted from a Humanistic Nursing Communication theoretical relationship statement can be stated as follows:

To the degree that the nursing staff receives humanizing communication from the nursing supervisor, to that degree the nursing staff will tend to be satisfied with the interpersonal communication with supervisor.

It is proposed that this tool may also be used appropriately with other theories within the holistic and humanistic perspective.

ADMINISTRATION

The JCSI Questionnaire requires about 15 minutes to complete. Using this instrument in a research project, it is relatively easily administered in pre-and post-test experimental procedures. Used as a data collection tool in a consulting context, the tool can readily be administered to large groups with minimal supervision, given written instructions. In association with research or consulting, it is important that the respondent's identity remain anonymous, yet that a process be used which allows one to remind tardy respondents to return the questionnaire. (See Sample Memo, attached.) Use of computer-scored forms can facilitate the data-gathering process and bypass keying data into the computer.

VALIDITY AND RELIABILITY

The JCSI has an internal consistency of .92 and test-re-test reliability ranging from .51 to .71. Additional analysis of the tool's reliability and validity is needed; it is recommended that validity and reliability analysis be completed for each specific research project until norms can be established.

ANALYSIS OF DATA

For consultation purposes, analysis of variance has been used as the primary statistical procedure to determine the relationship between health care supervisors and their staff's responses. Additional correlational studies can be done on demographic data and also on subsets of the scales as the findings indicate potentially relevant information.

In order to reduce the data to manageable proportions for research purposes, the items on the JCSI were analyzed to identify clusters of related items. Using principal components factor analysis with a decision rule requiring each factor to have an Eigenvalue greater than 1.00 resulted in six-factor solutions accounting for a high percentage of the total variance. See Tables 3 and 6. To attempt to interpret and describe the cluster of job-facet items forming each factor, descriptive factor titles were assigned. Each item was assigned to a factor only once. If a pre-post experimental design is used, the data can be analyzed by using "t" tests on pre-and post-factor difference scores. A negative mean will indicate that pretest scores are higher than post-test scores.

REFERENCES CITED

Carter, E. W., (1982). Stress in Nursing Students; Dispelling some of the myth. *Nursing Outlook*, April, 248-252.

Crino, M. E., and While, M. C., (1981). Satisfaction in communication: An examination of the Downs-Hazen measure. *Psychological Reports, 49*, 831-838.

Downs, Cal W. and Hazen, M. D. (1977). A factor analytic study of communication satisfaction. *Journal of Business Communication, 14*(3), 63-73.

Duldt, Bonnie Weaver Grant (1980). "Job/Communication Satisfaction/ Importance Survey Questionnaire," in: *Workshop Proposals, Speeches, and Other Unpublished Writings*. (Unpublished manuscript, registered copyright number TXU 49-169.)

Duldt, Bonnie Weaver (1987). *Improving staff nurses' skills in coping with other people's anger.* Unpublished research report available from author. Greenville, North Carolina: East Carolina University.

Duldt, Bonnie Weaver, and Giffin, Kim (1985). *Theoretical Perspectives for Nursing*, Boston: Little, Brown and Company.

Duldt, Bonnie Weaver, Giffin, Kim, and Patton, Bobby (1984). *Interpersonal Communication in Nursing*. Philadelphia: F. A. Davis, Co.

Ferguson, Vernice, (1988). Tipping the scales. Unpublished speech presented to the Sigma Theta Tau banquet of the Beta Nu and Theta Iota Chapters, Farmville, North Carolina, November 17, 1988.

Hersey, Paul, and Bonnie W. Duldt (1989). *Situational Leadership in Nursing*. East Norwalk, Conn.: Appleton-Lange.

Herzberg, Frederick, (1966). *Work and the nature of man* New York: Plenum.

Herzberg, F., Mausner, B., and Snyderman, B., (1959). *The motivation to work*. (2nd ed.) New York: Wiley.

Larson, E., Lee, P.C., Brown, M. A., and Shorr, J., (1984). Job satisfaction: assumptions and complexities. *Journal of Nursing Administration, 1984*(1), 31-38.

Likert, Rensis, (1967). *New Patterns of Management*. New York: McGraw-Hill.

Meissner, J. E., (1986). Nurses are we eating our young? *Nursing86*, March, 51-53.

Pfaff, J., (1987). Factors related to job satisfaction/dissatisfaction of registered nurses in long-term care facilities.

Pincus, J. D., (1986). Communication: Key contributor to effectiveness—the research. *Journal of Nursing Administration, 16*(9), 19-25.

Stewart, John, and D'Angelo, Gary (1975). *Together: Communicating Interpersonally* Reading, Mass.: Addison-Wesley Publishing Company, p 23.

Thiry, R. A., (1977). Relationship of communication satisfaction to need fulfillment among Kansas nurses. Unpublished doctoral dissertation, University of Kansas, 1977.

Relevant References

Buerhaus, Peter I. (2005). Six–Part series on the state of the RN workforce in the United States. *Nursing Economics*, 23(2), 58-69.

Buerhaus, P., Donelan, K., Ulrich, B., Des Roches, C., Normal, L., and Dittus, R. (2007). Impact of the nurse shortage on hospital patient care: Comparative perspectives. *Health Affairs*, 26(3), 853-62.

DuPlooy, Jocobus Christoffel. (2006). A comparative study of the levels of job satisfaction and communication satisfaction between the nursing staff of the psychiatric ward and the nursing staff of other wards at 1 military hospital. (Unpublished Master's Thesis.) Pretoria, South Africa: University of Limpopo, Medunsa Campus.

APPENDIX

Table 1. Eigenvalue, percent of variance and cumulative percent of Satisfaction Factors.

Factors	Eigenvalue	Percent of Variance	Cumulative Percent
1. Communication with Immediate Supervisor	9.00058	36.0	36.0
2. Job, Personal	3.12119	12.5	48.5
3. Communication with Co-workers	1.91606	7.7	56.2
4. Communication with Others	1.70374	6.8	63.0
5. Job, Organizational	1.37366	5.5	68.5
6. Leadership	1.05464	4.2	72.7

Table 2. Number of items and range of loadings for Satisfaction Factors.

	Factors	N	Range
1.	Communication with Immediate Supervisor	7	.67637-.91845
2.	Job, Personal	5	.60430-.80149
3.	Communication with Co-workers	4	.70745-.81350
4.	Communication with Others	3	.66529-.83078
5.	Job, Organizational	4	.48255-.82558
6.	Leadership	2	.70120-.76194

Table 3. Six Factor orthogonally rotated factor matrix of Satisfaction scores after rotation with Kiaser normalization.

Satisfaction Factors	Item Loadings

Factor 1. Communication with Immediate Supervisor

23. Immediate supervisor understands and listens to subject	.91845
20. Subject's communication with immediate supervisor.	.89667
21. Immediate supervisor's communication with subject.	.87342
19. Subject's relationship with immediate supervisor.	.85902
22. Recognition immediate supervisor gives for work.	.83800
24. Manner in which immediate supervisor gives direction and guidance to subject.	.83236
4. Communication from immediate supervisor regarding what is going on in general.	.67637

Factor 2. Job, Personal

9. Sense of achievement involved with work.   .80149

10. Challenge involved in work.   .77560

11. How well like work.   .72329

12. Use of abilities in work.   .65190

13. Training and experience provided in work.   .60430

Factor 3. Communication with Co-workers

16. Friendliness of fellow staff members.   .81350

18. Informal communication among nursing staff members.   .77272

15. Help provided by fellow staff members.   .73639

14. Interpersonal relationships among fellow staff members.   .70745

Factor 4. Communication with Others

27. Communication with physicians or equivalent.	.83078
28. Communications with a specific unit (Donor Recruitment, ARC; specific committee, hosp).	.75648
26. Communications with other departments within the agency.	.66529

Factor 5. Job, Organizational

8. Formal means of communication among the nursing staff (memos, notices, etc.).	.82558
5. Information received about nursing unit's goals and plans . . .	.70441
7. Information received about administrative policies affecting work.	.53639
6. Information received about staff accomplishments.	.48255

Factor 6. Leadership

25. Communications with the Director of the Dept. of Nursing (or equivalent).	.76194
17. Value of being associated with this nursing staff and health care agency.	.70120

Table 4. Eigenvalue, percent of variance and cumulative percent of Importance Factors

Factors	Eigenvalue	Percent of Variance	Cumulative Percent
1. Communication with Co-workers	9.36887	37.5	37.5
2. Communication with Supervisor, Personal	2.29495	9.2	46.7
3. Job, Personal	1.59056	6.4	53.0
4. Job, Organizational	1.53690	6.1	59.2
5. Communication with Supervisor, Organizational	1.20535	4.8	64.0
6. Communication with Others	1.09835	4.4	68.4

Table 5. Number of items and range of loadings for Importance Factors.

	Factors	N	Range
1.	Communication with Co-workers	4	.61813-.74338
2.	Communication with Supervisor, Personal	3	.75626-.81793
3.	Job, Personal	4	.53131-.82752
4.	Job, Organizational	6	.41398-.76971
5.	Communication with Supervisor, Organizational	5	.46362-.67901
6.	Communication with Others	3	.57955-.81159

Table 6. Six Factor orthogonally rotated factor matrix of Importance scores after rotation with Kiaser normalization.

Importance Factors	Item Loadings

Factor 1. Communication with Co-workers

18. Informal communication among the nursing staff members.	.74338
14. Interpersonal relationships among fellow staff members.	.70188
16. Friendliness of fellow staff members.	.66097
15. Help provided by fellow staff members.	.61813

Factor 2. Communication with Supervisor, Personal.

21. Immediate supervisor's communication with subject.	.81793
20. Subject's communication with immediate supervisor.	.80664
19. Subject's relationship with immediate supervisor.	.75628

Factor 3. Job, Personal

12. Use of abilities in work	.82752
10. Challenge involved in work.	.81817
9. Sense of achievement involved with work.	.72207
11. How well like work.	.53131

Factor 4. Job, Organizational

5. Information received about nursing unit's goals and plans.	.76971
7. Information received about administrative policies affecting work.	.65495
6. Information received about staff accomplishments.	.65241
4. Communication from immediate supervisor regarding what is going on in general	.61925
8. Formal means of communicating among nursing staff (memos, notices, etc.).	.56163
13. Training and experience provided in work.	.41398

Factor 5. Communication with Supervisor, Organizational

25. Communications with the Director
of the Department of Nursing (or   .67901
equivalent).

24. Manner in which immediate
supervisor gives direction and   .53109
guidance to subject.

23. Immediate supervisor understands
and listens to subject.   .51209

17. Value of being associated with this
nursing staff and health care agency.   .51071

22. Recognition immediate supervisor
gives for work.   .46362

Factor 6. Communication with Others

26. Communications with other
departments within the agency.   .81159

28. Communications with a specific unit
(Donor Recruitment, ARC; specific   .69650
committee, hospital).

27. Communication with physicians or
equivalent.   .57955

Table 7. Comparison of factors identified by investigators.

Herzberg (1959)	Downs & Hazen (1977)	Pincus (1986)	*Pfaff (1987)*	Thiry (1977)*
Motivating Factors or Satisfiers				
Achievement	Personal feedbacK	Communication with one's supervisor	Achievement	Communic. climate
Recognition	Corporate perspective.	Communication climate	Recognition	Personal feedback
Task	Organizational integration	Personal feedback	Task	Communication with supervisor
		Communication with top management		
Responsibility	Relations with one's supervisor	Organizational integration		Responsibility
				Media quality
Advancement	Communication climate in gen.	Media quality	Advancement	Organizational integration
		Communication with subordinates	Leadership	
	Horizontal communication	Horizontal communication		Horizontal communication
	Media quality	Organizational perspective		Communication with subordinates
	Relations with subordinates			Organizational perspective

Hygienic Factors or Dissatisfiers

Herzberg	*Pfaff*
Company policy	Facility policy
Administration	Current job environment
Supervision	
Salary	Salary
Interpersonal	Job security
Relations with Co-workers	Peer relations
Working Conditions	Supervisor & staff relationships.

---

* Nursing studies.

Subject No._____

JOB SATISFACTION AND COMMUNICATIONS SURVEY QUESTIONNAIRE

By

Bonnie W. Battey, R. N., Ph.D.

Instructions:

Questions requiring a response on a rating scale are to be answered by circling *one* of the numbers. The positive numbers indicate a positive attitude, evaluation, feeling, agreement, etc., and negative numbers indicate the opposite. The zero is to indicate a neutral attitude, not sure, or no opinion.

Questions regarding a written response are intended to be answered in 25 words or less.

Please DO NOT SIGN your name to this document: your identity is coded solely to enable us to follow people's responses over time. We need to know certain information which will be helpful in interpretation of your responses.

Please indicate your Occupational status: Gender:_____ Age:_____
        a. Supervisor. male_____
        b. Head Nurse. female_____
        c. Staff Nurse
        d. other_____.

Please indicate your current service assignment:_____

Proceed according to verbal instructions.

1. How satisfied are you in your present job?

   -3 -2 -1 0 +1 +2 +3

   Dissatisfied   Satisfied

2. How important is job satisfaction to you?

   -3 -2 -1 0 +1 +2 +3

   Unimportant   Important

3. How successful do you think you are in your job?

   -3 -2 -1 0 +1 +2 +3

   Unsuccessful   Successful

4. How do you feel about the communication from your supervisor about what is going on in general?

   -3 -2 -1 0 +1 +2 +3

   Dissatisfied   Satisfied

   -3 -2 -1 0 +1 +2 +3

   Unimportant   Important

5. How do you feel about the information you receive regarding your unit's goals and plans?

   -3 -2 -1 0 +1 +2 +3

   Dissatisfied   Satisfied

   -3 -2 -1 0 +1 +2 +3

   Unimportant   Important

6. How do you feel about the information you receive regarding staff accomplishments?

   -3 -2 -1 0 +1 +2 +3

   Dissatisfied   Satisfied

   -3 -2 -1 0 +1 +2 +3

   Unimportant   Important

7. How do you feel about the information you receive regarding administrative policies that affect your work group?

   -3 -2 -1 0 +1 +2 +3

   Dissatisfied   Satisfied

   -3 -2 -1 0 +1 +2 +3

   Unimportant   Important

8. How do you feel about the formal means of communication among the nursing staff, i.e., memos, notices, etc.

-3 -2 -1 0 +1 +2 +3

- -

Dissatisfied   Satisfied

-3 -2 -1 0 +1 +2 +3

- -

Unimportant   Important

9. How do you feel about the sense of achievement involved with your work?

-3 -2 -1 0 +1 +2 +3

- -

Dissatisfied   Satisfied

-3 -2 -1 0 +1 +2 +3

- -

Unimportant   Important

10. How do you feel about the challenge involved in your work?

-3 -2 -1 0 +1 +2 +3

- -

Dissatisfied   Satisfied

-3 -2 -1 0 +1 +2 +3

- -

Unimportant   Important

11. How do you feel about how well you like your work?

-3 -2 -1 0 +1 +2 +3

- -

Dissatisfied   Satisfied

-3 -2 -1 0 +1 +2 +3

- -

Unimportant   Important

12. How do you feel about the use of your abilities on this job?

-3 -2 -1 0 +1 +2 +3

Dissatisfied   Satisfied

-3 -2 -1 0 +1 +2 +3

Unimportant   Important

13. How do you feel about the training and experience provided by your job?

-3 -2 -1 0 +1 +2 +3

Dissatisfied   Satisfied

-3 -2 -1 0 +1 +2 +3

Unimportant   Important

14. How do you feel about the interpersonal relationships among the nursing personnel on your unit?

-3 -2 -1 0 +1 +2 +3

Dissatisfied   Satisfied

-3 -2 -1 0 +1 +2 +3

Unimportant Important

15. How do you feel about the help provided by your fellow staff members?

-3 -2 -1 0 +1 +2 +3

Dissatisfied   Satisfied

-3 -2 -1 0 +1 +2 +3

Unimportant   Important

16. How do you feel about the friendliness of your fellow staff members?

-3 -2 -1 0 +1 +2 +3

Dissatisfied   Satisfied

-3 -2 -1 0 +1 +2 +3

Unimportant   Important

17. How do you feel about the value of being associated with this nursing staff and health agency?

-3 -2 -1 0 +1 +2 +3

Dissatisfied   Satisfied

-3 -2 -1 0 +1 +2 +3

Unimportant   Important

18. How do you feel about the informal means of communication among the nursing staff members?

-3 -2 -1 0 +1 +2 +3

Dissatisfied   Satisfied

-3 -2 -1 0 +1 +2 +3

Unimportant   Important

19. How do you feel about your relationship with your immediate superior or supervisor?

-3 -2 -1 0 +1 +2 +3

Dissatisfied Satisfied

-3 -2 -1 0 +1 +2 +3

Unimportant Important

20. How do you feel about your communication with your immediate superior or supervisor?

--3 -2 -1 0 +1 +2 +3

Dissatisfied Satisfied

-3 -2 -1 0 +1 +2 +3

Unimportant Important

21. How do you feel about your immediate superior's or supervisor's communication with you?

-3 -2 -1 0 +1 +2 +3

Dissatisfied Satisfied

-3 -2 -1 0 +1 +2 +3

Unimportant Important

22. How do you feel about the recognition your immediate superior or
    supervisor gives you for your work?

    -3 -2 -1 0 +1 +2 +3

    Dissatisfied   Satisfied

    -3 -2 -1 0 +1 +2 +3

    Unimportant Important

23. How do you feel about the extent to which your immediate superior
    or supervisor seems to understand you and listen to you?

    -3 -2 -1 0 +1 +2 +3

    Dissatisfied   Satisfied

    -3 -2 -1 0 +1 +2 +3

    Unimportant   Important

24. How do you feel about the manner in which your immediate superior
    or supervisor gives you direction and guidance about how to perform
    your tasks?

    -3 -2 -1 0 +1 +2 +3

    Dissatisfied   Satisfied

    -3 -2 -1 0 +1 +2 +3

    Unimportant   Important

25. How do you feel about the communications with your Nursing Administrator?

-3 -2 -1 0 +1 +2 +3

Dissatisfied Satisfied

-3 -2 -1 0 +1 +2 +3

Unimportant   Important

26. How do you feel about the communications with other departments within the health agency?

-3 -2 -1 0 +1 +2 +3

Dissatisfied   Satisfied

-3 -2 -1 0 +1 +2 +3

Unimportant   Important

27. How do you feel about the communications with the physicians?

-3 -2 -1 0 +1 +2 +3

Dissatisfied   Satisfied

-3 -2 -1 0 +1 +2 +3

Unimportant   Important

28. How do you feel about the communications with the Volunteers?

-3 -2 -1 0 +1 +2 +3

- -

Dissatisfied   Satisfied

-3 -2 -1 0 +1 +2 +3

- -

Unimportant   Important

29. What factors do you think contribute most to your satisfaction on the job?

30. What factors do you think contribute most to your DISsatisfaction on the job?

31. What do you consider the most important aspect of your job?

32. What one change do you feel would help you become more satisfied with your job?

Please look over the questionnaire to be certain that you have responded to each scale and to all questions by marking one item only. Please place your completed questionnaire in a sealed envelope and give it to the designated person. Thank you for your participation.

SAMPLE MEMO

To: Nursing Service Personnel
From:*(Consultant's Name)*
Date:_____
Re: Job-Communications Satisfaction-Importance Survey

The administrative staff at *(Institution or agency)* has expressed concern about how satisfied employees are about their jobs and about the communication practices within the organization. I have agreed to conduct a survey to explore some facets of these things to determine if there is a problem and, if so, what it might be. If problems are found, I will make recommendations which may aid in initiating corrective actions by the administrative staff. The ultimate goal is to make you feel good about working at this agency.

While I am anxious that every precaution is taken to assure your individual responses will remain anonymous, it is hoped that the results can be reported according to groups within *(Institution or agency)*, i.e., according to job classification and according to each nursing unit. So, while you need not sign the questionnaire, I would like you to indicate the nursing unit to which you are assigned and whether you are an R.N., L.P.N., or a non-licensed nursing staff member.

In order that I can verify that you have responded, would you write your name on the attached index card and place it in the designated box when you deliver your completed questionnaire to the collection box located at _____. Your name will be checked off a list and, while all questionnaires remain unidentified, it will be possible to remind tardy ones to please turn in the questionnaire.

If you have any questions or would like clarification of some aspect of the survey, you may contact me as follows:_____ _____.

Please return the questionnaires by *date*. Your participation and cooperation is appreciated.

All of this may be helpful—to YOU!

NOTES

NOTES

ACKNOWLEDGEMENTS

There have been many of my friends, former students, and fellow faculty who have shared with me their thoughts about collegial relationships. Remembering many of those conversations has helped to develop this research tool to accompany Humanizing Nursing Communication Theory. This manual represents my sincere gratitude with the hope that it will be helpful in providing effective leadership and management in nursing practice.

www.ingramcontent.com/pod-product-compliance
Lightning Source LLC
Chambersburg PA
CBHW021929170526
45157CB00005B/2244